Of Loss and Love
A Journey of the Heart

by

Suzanne Harman Munson

www.OakleaPress.com

Of Loss and Love—a Journey of the Heart © 2023 by Suzanne Harman Munson, all rights reserved. No part of this book may be used or reproduced in any manner whatsoever without written permission except in the case of brief quotations embodied in critical articles and reviews. For information visit The Oaklea Press, www.oakleapress.com.

Interior artwork by Erin Cook
Cover by James A. Jernigan

Author: Suzanne Harman Munson: suzmunson01@gmail.com
Artist: Erin Cook: ErinN2art@aol.com

CONTENTS

Prologue 4

The Early Journey 5

Things Dear 20

Alone 27

Holidays 33

Living Well 40

Journeys in the Natural World 54

Journeys of the Mind 69

A New Journey Unfolds 74

Prologue: The Journey

After a great loss, every heart follows its own pathway, its own personal journey. Some hearts bend, never to become whole again. Others mend.

The reflections in his book trace my path toward healing and renewal after the loss of my husband Ned, following a long and good marriage. I was suddenly alone, and I had to find a new way of living.

After Ned's death, I began to have new insights that I wanted to express on paper. The reflections began with an idea that seemed important, a thought that needed to be developed, an image from my window or walks. When I felt an insight "coming on," I quickly found a yellow note pad and let the words flow.

The first pieces reflect the period of early widowhood, the days of raw hurt and loss. Next came a time to embrace living, to dwell in the moment, to enjoy life's small and large gifts. And the last words were written when a new partner miraculously came into my world.

I don't consider myself a professional poet. The words do not follow a particular pattern or cadence. Rather, these reflections are a form of journaling—a transcript of my personal journey.

I have shared these writings with family and friends, and they have encouraged me to publish, to communicate with a wider audience. I hope that my journey in some way will comfort and encourage others who seek light and solace.

The Early Journey

In the weeks after Ned's funeral in February, I was busy with the business of death—insurance papers, thank-you notes, banking details. I had always loved the first glorious days of spring, but one fine day in April, I recalled T.S. Eliot's glum opening lines in the "Waste Land."

April

He said that April
is the cruelest month.
I thought that strange
until today.

February covered my heart
in a soft gray mist,
burned away
on this radiant spring day.

I am not ready to
celebrate life this day,
to hear sweet sounds
of birds with mates,
to witness the glory
of gardens and skies,

to stride along with
a skip in my step,
to revel in the wonder
of green growing things.

Of Loss and Love

It is all too much for me
this golden day.
I turn away,
I turn within,
I look for solace
in a soft gray space.

Our family gravesite is in Hollywood Cemetery, a historic Virginia landscape of peace and beauty. Gradually, I realized that my relationship with the place had changed.

The Grave Tender

I always admired
the cemetery,
its ancient gray marbles
and venerable old trees.

But it was always
a place for others,
for others' hearts and memories.

I was only visiting.

Now I am a grave-tender,
a care-giver of graves.
I soften his place
with sprigs of spruce
and water when days are dry.

I clean the leaves
from his parents' space
and see where I will lie.

On his birthday,
we bring flowers.
I remove them
when they die.

Of Loss and Love

I note the names
on graves nearby,
neighbors forever
as seasons drift on,
still and calm
under an eternal sky.

We feel the loss of a spouse on many levels—the loss of friendship, of support during our dark hours, of physical companionship. As the weeks wore on, there was a physicality to my loneliness. I wrote this piece on vacation by myself at a mountain retreat.

Skin

I miss the lover's touch.
My skin has been
asleep so long.

I lounge in a deck chair
above a cobalt lake.
A couple suns below me,
peaceful, relaxed,
from seasons of compatibility.
Tonight, they will sleep
skin to skin.

I take in the scene:
flaxen-green timothy fields,
August-blue skies,
sunny goldenrod,
cotton-white clouds,
a farmer's russet barn,
a vine-draped wagon wheel.

I am keen to the
sense of sight.
I have lapsed
my sense of feel.

Of Loss and Love

My hands run down the
warm arm of the chair,
through the length of my hair,
and over my body,
as I begin
to awake again,
to honor my skin
with a lover's touch.

At night, I often looked at the sky and wondered where Ned was and what he was doing. I sensed that he was still alive, but just in another dimension that I could not access. Some people have little or no curiosity about what happens to us after we die, or more accurately, after we leave physical form. Others deride any attempt to explore the afterlife, leaving this to the realm of kooks and mystics.

I was different. I wanted to know everything there is to know about the progress of the soul, or to use less loaded terminology, the evolution of human consciousness. I augmented wisdom from religious texts with recent scientific research, particularly studies of the profound, life-altering lessons provided now from near-death experience reports. I must have read more than three dozen books on the subject.

In this regard, I believe that spiritually and intellectually, we are where our ancestors were in the Middle Ages, when everyone believed that the world was flat and that the sun revolved around the earth. They simply couldn't conceive of an alternate view of the universe.

Today, there is an explosion of information—gathered by medical doctors, university researchers, psychologists, and others—about life after physical death. For those with open minds, our world view is changing rapidly and profoundly.

The Bookshelf

I put novels aside
the day he died.
I didn't want fiction.

I wanted to know the truth
about where he had gone.

I read books about
those who died
and then returned.
They do not lie
about what they learned.

Of Loss and Love

I sought the wisdom of mediums,
psychics, and mystics,
about parallel dimensions
and quantum physics,
the universe deep and wide,
the fluid nature of our spirits,
and what it's like on the Other Side.

I learned of connection
with all living things,
on all living planes,
and after we roam,
the place called Home.

I cleared a space
for these new texts,
my Cosmic Bookshelf.

This is where I confirmed
my view of God and
why we are here.

It is all very simple.
God is love.
We are here
to learn to love.
Nothing else matters.
Our matter does not matter.

We are souls
encased in bodies,
waiting to be free.
He is free
and is waiting for me.
He is loving life
on the Other Side.

Betty J. Eadie published one of the most widely read, early books on the afterlife, setting the stage for thousands of similar near-death experience (NDE) accounts to follow in other books and online. The NDE phenomenon is now an established field of study by serious academic and medical researchers. I took great interest in what she wrote about her experience in the next dimension, in her glimpse of life after physical death.

She said that she wanted to learn the purpose of life on the earth—why are we here? She was shown that love is supreme, that without love we are nothing. We are here to help each other, to care for each other, to understand, forgive, and serve one another. Anything that we do to show love is worthwhile: a smile, a word of encouragement, a small act of sacrifice. Everything else is meaningless unless it is done for the benefit of others. Our gifts and talents are given to us to help us serve. And in serving others, we grow spiritually.

Some of the books that I read dealt with the "death with dignity" movement, which fortunately had taken hold by the time that Ned died of cancer. No longer do families feel obligated, even shamed into, having their terminally ill loved ones tied to tubes and filled with noxious chemicals in a sterile hospital room, on life support until the hour of death.

We faced the choice of one last hurrah—wracking his disease-riddled body with yet more harsh chemo treatment in the hospital—or greeting the inevitable by taking him home in hospice for a peaceful passage, surrounded by family. I wrote this piece several months after the funeral.

The Bed

I sit where he left us,
in the family den,
bright, full of light,
with a fold-out bed,
navy blue, his favorite color.

Of Loss and Love

When he came home
on a stretcher,
true to form,
he thought of others,
asked the crew
if they'd like a coca cola.

I refused to order
the single kind
of hospital bed.
That would not do.
It was lonely.

He never liked
being alone.
He would not
be alone now.

I pulled out
the double sofa bed.

We kept his vigil,
two at a time,
one nearby and one in the bed,
his out-of-town children
first on the watch.

He slept mostly,
sometimes saying funny things.
We wrote them down.
In the middle of the night,
he cried for a hug.
His children
covered him with love.

Of Loss and Love

We couldn't anticipate
the moment of his passing,
what day, what hour.
Was it chance
our minister came by
at that very time?

With kind respect,
he gave
the last rites,
a strong voice,
full of force,
words of release,
as we surrounded the bed.

As the spirit of
the one we loved
left home,
we knew
if there is such a thing
as a good death,
he had experienced one.

Everyone in the family grieved in his or her own way. The loss of a husband is naturally very different from the loss of a father or brother. We all shed our tears, in our own times and places. Grief, after all, is the price of love. I made new friends in a grief support group.

Tears

Tears come in
unexpected places,
sometimes quietly
in public spaces.

Let them fall.
Our feelings
nourish healing.

Grief is only love,
with no place to go.

One man in mourning
for his wife
goes to a pool.
He finds relief,
releasing his grief,
tears under water,
where people cannot see.

Hearing
an old love song
on his car radio,
he noticed a woman
in her car.
She was crying also.
Somehow,
he felt connected.

Of Loss and Love

Let the tears flow.
We are really crying
for ourselves,
in our fears.

The one we mourn
has no tears,
content to abide
free from care
on the Other Side.

At night, I began to watch with fascination a popular medium on TV. Several friends had consulted mediums, connecting with their loved ones with remarkable and deeply meaningful results. I wondered what it was like to have a "spirit spouse," to know that your mate is still in communion with you, although unseen.

The Spirit Spouse

Three million people
each week
watch a medium
on TV,
connecting the living
with loved ones
they seek,
channeling spirit husbands
with living wives,
and spirit wives
with living husbands.

Reunions are amazing
to behold,
full of feeling
and precise detail,
bringing insight
and healing
as messages unfold.

One wonders—
what is it like
to have a spirit spouse?

Mediums say our spirits
enjoy being with us.

Of Loss and Love

They join us for
birthdays and weddings.
They sit at our table
on Thanksgiving Day.
They know when
a baby is on the way.

Spirit spouses
demand very little—
no meals, no laundry,
no needs of any kind.

All they wish
is to be remembered
from time to time.
All they want
is to see us happy.

When we are
joined by love,
our loved ones
never leave us.

They're in heaven,
but in a sense,
we are their heaven.

Things Dear

      When not exploring metaphysical questions, I thought a great deal about the physical things that Ned left behind—his clothes, his books, his car. Many find comfort in retaining articles of clothing and other reminders of their loved ones. I gave a number of Ned's things to family and charity but kept others.

Things Dear

Places and things
remain unchanged
since the hour he left.

His dresser still holds
t-shirts and socks,
the cufflinks box.

His children took
some shirts and belts,
saving these,
in their own ways,
for comfort
on lonesome days.

There are coats
in the closet,
shoes on the floor,
ties in a rack
on the
bedroom door.

Of Loss and Love

I have given
many things
away to the poor.
There will be time
to let go of more.

For now, I hold to
things that are dear.
I just like
having them here.

The Sweater

In the fall,
as days drew cold,
I looked through
his sweaters,
worn and old.

The gray one
was special,
with garage grease,
a small moth hole.

I picked it up
from where it lay.
A classic:
"Made in the USA."

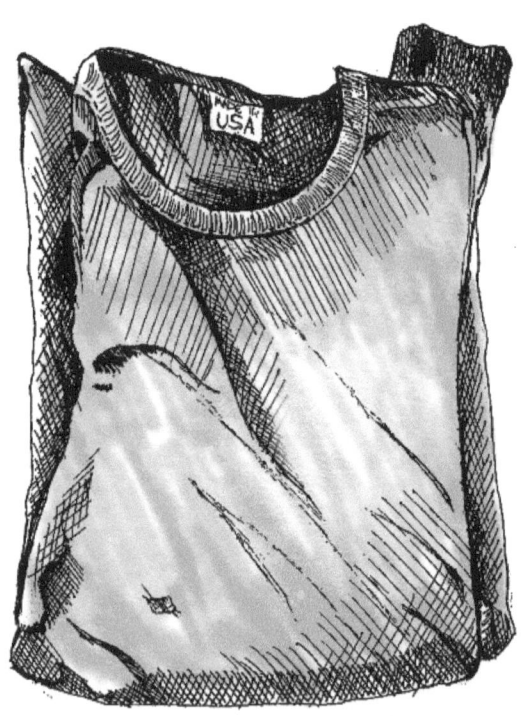

I heard that the living
find comfort in
clothes worn
by departed ones.
I decided to give
the sweater a try.

Like his spirit,
it was warm and comfortable,
traditional and durable.
I could have returned it
to its drawer,
but I kept it out instead.

Of Loss and Love

At night, I place it
on his side of the bed.
In the morning,
I take it where I stay.

Am I crazy?
Maybe.
But I do it anyway.

While we keep certain things that remind us of those who have passed on, we must let go of others. Ned's old green van needed repairs and was dangerous to drive. We had bought it years earlier for carpool to school. He drove it to work and graciously gave me the better car to take to my job.

The Used Car Lot

I never thought of CarMax
as a place for tears.
But, oddly,
it is.

It's where we say goodbye
to memories,
of rides to the beach,
to work, to school,
of birthdays, cotillions,
and trips to the pool.

The van was part
of his identity,
stable, modest,
and sturdy.

This piece of metal
was a piece
of our lives.

The sales lady found a tissue
and waited for me
to stop.
She said that tears
are often shed
on this used car lot.

Of Loss and Love

I signed the bill
of sale today.
I watched as they
drove the van away.
I wonder—
was it sad too?

In the early morning, I often sit on the terrace at home and absorb the sun. Usually, my eyes are drawn to a particular tree.

Ned's Tree

I look at the tree
my husband saved
from K-Mart years ago.

It was a spindly sapling,
thirsty, limp, and low,
an end-of-summer bargain,
an orphan needing a home.

He made a place for it,
watered it, watched it grow.
Today, it stands tall,
full to the sun,
straight and strong.

A large oak once
occupied that space.
It crushed our house
in a summer gust.

Ned's tree is a maple—
supple, graceful,
pliant in the wind,
roots deep in the earth,
a sentinel.

It will bend
with every storm,
and it will never
harm our home.

Alone

As time passed, I experienced a range of feelings about living alone. There were hours when I enjoyed peace and freedom in quietness. At other times, I was terribly lonely.

Lonely Hunter

The Heart is a Lonely Hunter,
the title of a book
I have not read.

A lovely line,
but only
a literary phrase
until I entered
this strange phase.

Now I find the words
on my mind
much of the time.

My heart is searching
for something
it cannot see,
for something
meant for me.

I am half
what I used to be.

Of Loss and Love

Is this the way
of days
to the end?

Or will
my soul
find another
friend?

I wonder.
Will I always
be a hunter?

After the funeral, my family returned to their homes. I realized that it had been more than three decades since I had lived entirely by myself.

Alone

It has been so long
since I've lived alone.
It seems unnatural.

Once two hearts
lodged here,
now one.

I think we weren't
designed to be alone.

Once we lived in
family-filled places.
Now we dwell
singly,
in empty spaces.

No one hears
our footsteps
in the hall.
No one hears us
if we call,
or fall.

We look outside
at the waning moon.
We phone a friend,
we play a tune.
We go to a movie,
then to a play,
We return alone.

Of Loss and Love

I read that a quarter of us
now live this way.
It's the new normal.
We must adjust.

At other times, I embraced my solitude.

Alone.
Yet, I don't feel alone.
There is a warm
presence here,
indefinable and not
quite tangible.

Are there friendly
spirits here?
Am I enveloped
in some form of love?
I think so.

But then,
how am I to know?

I have only to feel,
to conceive,
and then
to believe.

Although my home had a warm feel, the house next door often seemed forlorn. Once filled with friendly neighbors, it stayed empty for months. One winter day, I thought that the house looked especially melancholy:

The Neighbor's Window

My neighbor's upstairs window
stares at the morning,
empty and dark,
like the eye
of a soulless being.

I can tell the room
holds no chair,
no bed,
no pictures of family—
just empty.

No one lives
next door anymore.
No one loves
the house.
No one is there
to love me.

Just a vacant,
lonely space,
waiting to find its soul.

Alone in my car, I often station-surfed—from one musical genre to another. In earlier times, the music usually served just as background to my random thoughts. In my own new station in life, I began to listen with a different kind of attention.

Love Songs

I never knew
there were so many
love songs
on the radio.

Now I listen
with a different ear.
They are all
I seem to hear.

Tunes play
throughout the day
about new love,
love lost, love found.

It must be true
what they say—
Love makes the
world go 'round.

You never know
until yours
has gone away.

Holidays

Holidays, birthdays, and anniversaries during the first year of loss are problematic. February 14 came first for me.

Valentine's Day

Valentine's Day,
a week after the funeral.
I walked to the university
and along the way
stopped at the circular steps.

A student saw me,
from her place above,
my shoulders flagging.
She drew near
to give a hug.

We sat under
an old pine tree,
and she asked to
say a prayer with me.
She was lonely too.

Neighbors brought cupcakes,
the most delicious kind.
Friends called,
good thoughts in mind.
Children phoned
from far away.
Others came by
to stay.

Of Loss and Love

How sweet it is,
at the end of the day,
to feel some love
on Valentine's Day.

The three winter holidays—Thanksgiving, Christmas, and New Year's Eve—have been described as "The Bermuda Triangle" for those in emotional distress. Everyone else seems happy and engaged, while we sit in our pain. The spiritual journey that I had begun earlier, however, somehow sustained me during the cheery build-up toward Christmas.

Carols

I used to change stations
when Christmas songs
were playing.
I found them irritating.

This year,
I hear them differently.

Seers say that
music is for healing,
reflecting what
our hearts are feeling.

My heart is soft and open
this season.
I like the carols.
There must be a reason.

There's an old jazz song, "What are you doing New Years, New Year's Eve?" For singles with no one special at hand, this can be a sensitive question. I've never wanted to be alone on New Year's Eve, and when this holiday arrives, I think of a friend who had difficulty making commitments with the women in his life.

New Year's Eve

I knew a man
who danced
two women
through the
seasons
on strings
of affection.

New Year's Eve came,
the loneliest
time of the year
for a girl
in need
of cheer.

How did
the man
make his plan?
What did he say
to the one
left behind?

Did his string
of promises
snap
on that
special night?

Of Loss and Love

A lesson perhaps.

When the game
is up,
when you seek to be loved,
to believe,
it all boils down to
New Year's Eve.

Thanksgiving and Christmas for me were filled with family and good cheer, despite our loss earlier in the year. Alone again after the holidays, I felt a sense of letdown. The sun seemed to set too soon, and following the bustle of Christmas, activity slowed to a sedentary pace.

Winter Afternoons

Sometimes,
there is
a certain wistfulness
in a late
January day.

I watch at the window
as the sun shafts
its weak light
through barren trees,
as it pales and grays
and fades to the west.

There is a vagueness
in the air,
a soft longing,
a languor,
a reminiscence, a nostalgia,
a dreaminess, an abstraction,
a quiet melancholia.

The holidays are over.
Christmas trees peek
from cans along the street.

Of Loss and Love

Angels, crèches, and Santa's
sleep in their boxes
until December,
when the house
again beams bright,
flowing with family.

It is dusk now.
I remove the last
yule candle
from the sill.
I leave the window,
to turn
on a light.

Living Well—The Journey Continues

After the early period of grieving, I knew that I needed to take steps to embrace life—my life. I made new friends, traveled, engaged in meaningful volunteer work, and began to do some serious writing.
I absorbed messages about mindfulness, living in the moment, and savoring all of the senses that our Creator gives us to enjoy—taste, sound, touch, smell, sight.

The Sandwich

I made a summer sandwich,
a sensation of the season,
with the plumpest
juicy red tomato,
the smoothest
creamy mayonnaise,
and the thinnest
fine white toast.

I prepared it carefully
slicing it just right.
Then I rushed it
to its finish.

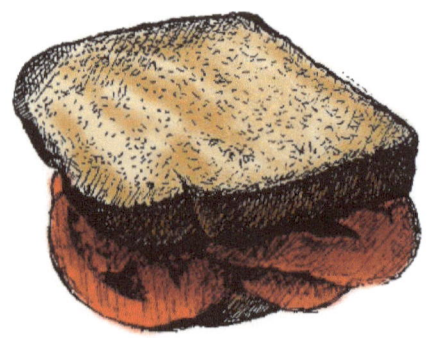

Soon, I wanted it back.

I forgot to
savor it,
slowly,
mindfully,
deliciously,
to enjoy every
sweet sensation,
as I scurried through
nature's lovely gift.

Of Loss and Love

Isn't that life?

We rush it down.
Then we wish
our days were back,
to savor slowly,
mindfully,
deliciously,
to relive those
lovely hours
that we mindlessly
let slip away.

The gift of touch. With the loss of a mate comes the loss of physical connectivity—a hand held, a kiss on the cheek, a snug presence under the sheets on a cold night.

Warm Towels

I gather warm towels
from the dryer
and hold them to my heart.

They are the closest thing
to a warm embrace
that I will have today.

Cozy towels are given
to baby animals
whose mothers have died.
Cotton comfort,
not real.

But in the absence
of real,
warm towels
have a lovely feel.

Reflecting further on the gift of touch, our skin is the largest organ of our body, but usually we just give it surface attention and neglect its underlying powers. Except for blemishes, bruises, and cuts, we tend to take this marvelous covering of our bodies for granted.

Our skin is filled with millions of sensory cells, exquisitely sensitive to a light, loving touch. How fortunate most of us are to have baths with clean running water at any temperature and tempo we desire. Yet, we usually treat our morning shower as a duty, rather than an experience to be enjoyed. This can be an opportunity to say "hello" to ourselves, to feel alive, from top to toes in a gentle water massage, living in the present moment, loving the present moment.

THE SHOWER

Wake,
Shower,
Fix on day.
Armpits.
Mindless minutes.

Pause,
Forget,
Focus,
Feel.

Warm fingerlings
massage
tired scalp,
the never-still brain.

Pity-pat rain
on arid back,
Happy little rivulets,
legs to toes.

Of Loss and Love

Cheeks into mist,
eyes closed.

Pause,
Enjoy,
A mindful minute.

The gift of sight. Even with perfect vision, we are often blind to the beauty that envelops us.

Sunsets

The sunset was spectacular,
splashes of gold
and pink and coral
across a sapphire sky.

I was busy.
I paused
to try to store
the sight,
to pull it
from memory
later,
when there
was time.

But we can never really
store a sunset
in all of its
vibrance
and passing
splendor.

Each sunset is here
only once
and will not appear
again.

Of Loss and Love

Tomorrow, I will
linger longer,
pausing on
the run,
to absorb the
passing vision
of clouds and sky
and sun.

And I will
try to learn
to treasure
those fleeting,
radiant
moments.

One day, I stood by a window observing a summer storm, and there seemed to be a message in its intensity and purpose.

SHARDS OF LIGHT

I watch the rain
come in.

Wind dances
the leaves of summer.
Thunder clouds,
the color of iron,
run low.

Earth's damp, spongy
scent rises.

I see a slash
of lightening and
move away from
the window.

Lightening serves
a grand purpose,
I have learned.

It charges clouds and rain
with nutrients,
nourishment for
our wide, green land.

Perhaps life's shards
of lightening,
those that pierce our
solitary hearts,
serve a wider, bolder
purpose, too.

In the fall, I absorb the beauty of the season.

AFTERNOON GOLD

It is November,
the days of afternoon gold.

Beyond my garden,
the sun slides west,
through gilded leaves,
against an indigo sky.

Our trees cling
to their glorious gowns
until the next sweep of rain
and cool rush of wind.

My eyes fasten on the
fleeting autumn palette,
jades, mustards, and russets.
Mother Nature's last great party
before retiring for her long siesta.

The gift of sound, the gift of music, balm for the soul long before David played the lyre to soothe Saul's troubled spirit. I surround myself with beautiful music to mute life's aggravations.

I am a news hound, intensely interested in politics and government. But there are times, more often now, when I must shut the world off during the day and find peace.

Solace

I shun irritations
today.
No unnerving news,
no TV, texts,
annoying views.

Music is my
companion now.
My healer,
my friend.

As I commence
my tasks,
calmness flows within.

The gift of scent. "Stop and smell the roses"— how often we fail to follow that simple admonition, on so many different levels. During a visit to the countryside, I came across a lavender farm, beginning my love affair with this divine scent. I say "divine" with some consideration, after reading *Appointments with Heaven* by Reggie Anderson, M.D.

Lavender

Last May,
I saw a lovely field
of lavender
and saved a stem
of fragrance
from that
splendid sunny day.

Today,
I explore its essence,
its ancient balm
and soothing presence.

A kindly country doctor
sits with patients
at their souls' passage.
He says that when
the curtain parts,
there is a breath
of citrus and lavender.

Today, I looked for
small green plants
to soften the
somber stone
in our family plot.

Of Loss and Love

I looked and looked,
then I saw
the lavender.

Tonight, the house
is filled with
its bouquet.
Tomorrow, it will
edge his grave.

Lavender will bend
with the wind
and grow in the rain.
It will sweeten
each breeze
that brushes his stone.

When winter arrived, with it came old, familiar scents.

DRIFTS

I step outside to
a cold, gray day.
A damp dusk descends
in the neighborhood.

In the air is the drift
of a wood fire.
I pause to breathe
its essence.

Familiar, smoky, inviting,
Primal, elemental,
Resonant of ancient fires
set against frosts,
fears, and shadows.

A neighbor has fed the flames,
someone I don't know.

Perhaps other neighbors
share in misty memories too,
of cooking fires and camp fires,
of songs and s'mores,
and kumbaya—
or maybe just
a comfy family den.

The scent connects.

Of Loss and Love

A pioneer said that
it was time to move
when he could smell
a neighbor's wood smoke.

On this night,
I reflect on the
communal closeness
of my neighbor's cozy fire.

Journeys in the Natural World

Nature has a great curative influence. Surrounded as we are by concrete and glass, we need to give our souls a nature bath when possible. I often walk at a retreat center, a sylvan landscape edging suburbia.

Unseen

I took a walk
across my favorite
field today.

The day was windy,
mild.
The wind was strong,
yet soft.
A Goldilocks day—
just right.

I felt the breeze
pass across
my face
and through
my hair.

I watched
as it rippled
the leaves
of a great oak.

I saw it lift the wing
of a coasting hawk.

Of Loss and Love

Yet, who can
see the wind?
No one.
But it is there.
A metaphor, perhaps.

Who has seen God?
Not I.
But I see
evidence
of His presence.

I have seen the Father
caress his children,
bend them,
heal them,
straighten them.

Like the wind,
unseen.
But there.

During another walk in this special place, I concluded that I had morphed into a proverbial tree-hugger.

The Tree Hugger

I used to smile
when they talked about
the tree huggers,
Don Quixotes
of the woods.

Youthful lovers
of old living things,
defenders of timbers,
young bodies pressed
against ancient bark,
daring men with saws
to make their mark.

I understand now.
A tree of fifty years
is a special thing.
A tree of one thousand
links with eternity.

Some trees are made
for raising houses,
others for nourishing souls.

I love the old gnarled things,
whipped by winter winds,
nuzzled by May breezes,
opening their world-worn
arms to me.

Of Loss and Love

Lately I have learned
that we are all related,
all wed
in the subatomic
energy field
of Nature's
worldwide web.

We are kindred spirits,
linked by physics
in cosmic ways we cannot see.

I took a walk in the country today.
It was a lonely time
to think and feel,
a necessary time to heal.
I followed a solitary trail
along streams and
valleys and fields.

The forest seemed to beckon me.
And, alone in my reverie,
free to do
a childish thing,
with no one watching,
I gently hugged a tree.

I also like to walk around a lake near my house. I was there on December 21st, one of my favorite days.

The Winter Solstice

Like a pagan,
I await the winter solstice,
the darkest day of the year.

I watch the weak sun disappear
behind the lake's bare trees,
dusky shadows in its wake.

Tomorrow, the sun shines stronger.
I watch its light grow longer,
inch by inch, until summer's solstice
when days again begin to fade.

I like winter.
Nature rests, its seeds already sown.
I rest, too.
No need to mow the lawn.

My garden sleeps until the vernal equinox
when nature leaps alive.
At the new moon, I too revive.
But for now, I just cocoon.

I spent several delightful summer weeks at Nimrod Hall, a rustic writers' retreat in rural Bath County, Virginia, a place very dear to my heart.

A Place in the Country

I've always longed for
a place in the country,
to visit, not to own.
Owning is too cumbersome.

A place with hills
and meadows and streams,
where I could wander
and ponder my dreams,
a simple space to stay
to nurture my heart
in nature's way.

I have found it here.
Nature is in its core,
in every pore,
feeding, cradling,
cultivating,
a place to paint, to write,
to laze in the sun,
gloriously away
from life on the run.

Colors are special here,
yellow finches on the rise,
soaring azure skies,
white mist at sunrise,
green, green everywhere.

Of Loss and Love

I breathe in the beauty and
for a day at least,
my roaming heart
is at peace.

A small river runs near the writers' retreat house. I always take time for a dip in the afternoons while visiting.

Dragonflies

The little river ran
quiet and clear.

I floated alone,
under leafy green arches
and summer-blue skies,
my legs to the sun.

Dragonflies soon found them,
first one couple,
then another, then a cluster,
lighting in tandem
on my knees,
wings brushed
with cobalt luster.

I took them as a sign,
a tender visit
just for me,
on this day of
lonely longing,
in my summer reverie.

No, the campers told me,
they're just the
old country couples,
dirty dancing
on your knees,
making love
before everyone,
pretty as you please,
ancient as the river,
fleeting as the breeze.

The *kumbaya* magic of this agreeable rural refuge continued, as some of us wrote of our Nimrod Hall experiences.

The Peaceable Kingdom

Ours is a peaceable
kingdom on the hill,
a place where
kindred spirits come,
from days long gone.

In the arms of
nature Mother,
we learn day by day
to open our hearts
to one another.

A harmless brown spider
lives in my room.
When I arrived,
we eyed each other,
he from his perch and
I from my place.
I decided that we
could share the space.

Today in the stubby grass,
a neighborly black snake
circled by.
He makes his home
under our house,
we learned.

Of Loss and Love

We watched
as he returned,
he to dwell beneath
and we above.

We live and
let live here,
as we will,
in our peaceful
kingdom on the hill.

My writing took me to other retreats from the highlands to the shore. I wrote two pieces at the ocean.

The Sea

I decided to engage
the waves today.
Before,
I lounged on the shore,
keeping my hair dry.

I wanted to feel
twelve years old again,
free and fearless
and full of verve.

I entered the water
slowly, cautiously,
braced against the cold,
sand and shells
shifting underfoot.

The surf slapped my body,
first calves, then knees,
then thighs.
I staggered, kept moving
farther into the sea.

Soon the waves and I
were fully engaged.

I bucked them,
dove through and under them,
rode them, and mastered them,
until reaching
the peaceful place.

Of Loss and Love

Here I lie,
eyes to the sky,
hair floating
with the tide,
ears tuned to
the undulating music
of eternal sea.

All of my life
I have bucked
the waves.

Now I dwell
in the lovely
quiet space beyond.

During my walks along the beach, I stop to watch the children at play.

Sandcastles

On the shore
in the morning,
children
bring shovels and buckets
and build with care
castles with towers
and spires in the air.

Other children come
at noon
and bully
the castles
down
into the sand,
until mere
heaps remain.

The way of the world.

We create cities
and civilizations,
only to see
bullies grown
to tyrants,
who distress,
destroy,
spoil,
and shatter.

Of Loss and Love

Meanwhile,
the sea
returns
to wash
the shore clean.

And tomorrow,
the children
will bring
buckets and shovels,
and they will begin
to build again.

While connecting with the natural world as much as possible, I made sure that my interior space, my home, expressed a sense of pleasure and peace. I furnished it with happy colors and added fresh new touches to fading areas. It was amazing how a simple twenty-dollar purchase improved my spirits.

The Curtain

My shower cover
grew old and sad,
its once-bright colors
now run drab.

A first sight
in the morning,
and the last at night,
it began to depress.

I found
a fresh drape
a new kind,
sunny, merry,
a fabulous find.

Amazing that
something so simple
can revive the mind.

Journeys of the Mind

My time alone provided hours for reflection, particularly about living with a sense of thankfulness.

Gratitude

We should be mindful
of how we spend
our head time.

We are
what we think.

Thankful thoughts
summon contentment,
erase self-pity,
resentment.

Emotions are like magnets,
attracting success or failure.
A simple law of Nature.

Negativity makes us sick,
shortens the wick
of our lives.

We practice an
attitude of gratitude
by saying thanks for small things:
a roof overhead,
a clean soft bed,
a shower in the morning,
a flower from the garden.

Of Loss and Love

We reflect on the big things:
health, family and friends,
our spiritual journey.

Soon,
the baseless things we fear
will simply disappear.

When I transitioned from the workplace to retirement, I wanted to recalibrate my thinking.

An Empty Head

When I left my last job,
I asked God to give me
an empty head.

My negative thoughts
were reeling
like a gerbil on a wheel.

I wanted a peaceful
psyche instead,
leaving niggling
thinking behind.

Now, my head is clear.

I listen with
an ear
for guidance.
I watch with
a thankful eye.

I say grace
for the grace
in my life today.

As I adjusted to life alone, I realized that for optimal mental health, I needed to stay engaged, active, and connected with others. It became important to give to others, including those outside of my economic circle, outside of my level of social comfort. I knew that isolation would be the first step down the road toward self-pity and self-absorption.

Out of Ourselves

It's easy to feel low
when we're
living slow.

Inaction slides
into depression,
spiritual suppression.

Poor me—
Pour me a drink.

We need to
jump-start our days,
move off the pity pot,
give thanks for
what we've got,
relieve ourselves
of the bondage of self.

Even when alone,
we don't have
to be lonely.
Unless we
want to be.

Of Loss and Love

Call friends.
Call those with no friends.
Volunteer.
Share kindness,
Send a card,
Give time.

It is only in giving
of ourselves
that we receive,
the strongest tonic
for those who grieve.

A New Journey Unfolds

Although I had always considered myself a completely independent woman, as time went by, I felt incomplete. Once part of a whole relationship, I felt "half." An important part of myself was missing—the part that is designed to love another. I envied people like this man and wife:

Hearts At One

I read about an
old married couple,
hospitalized,
at the end of
their lives,
in separate rooms,
side by side.

On their monitors,
nurses noticed
a phenomenon.

The couple's hearts
beat as one.

When one heart surged,
the other ensued.
When one was calm,
the other rested.
When one heart died,
the other soon followed.

Hearts in harmony—
the way things
should be.

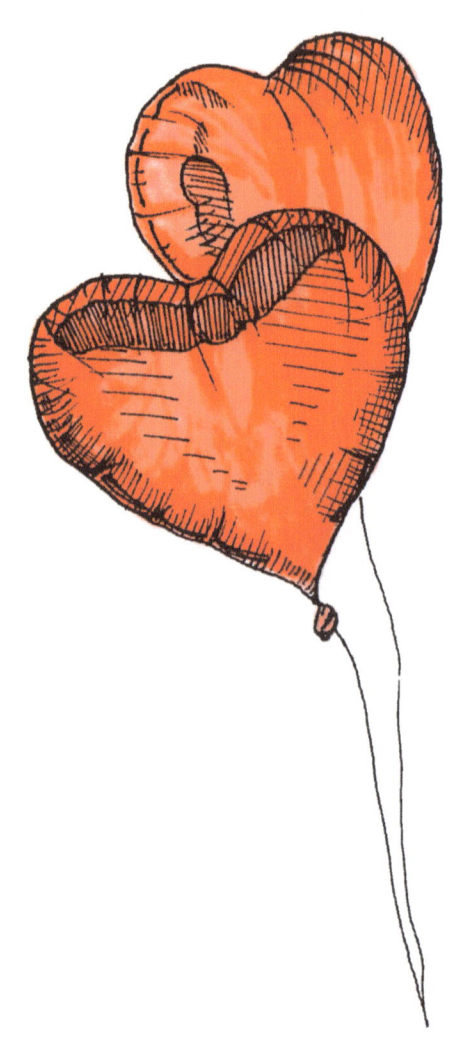

Of Loss and Love

How wonderful
for that couple,
never apart,
to share the
secret of life
in the beat
of a heart.

A good friend who became a widow said it best: that while she wasn't lonely in the usual sense—she lived an active life—her inner aloneness came from the realization that she was no longer truly special to someone, to a mate. She had lost the companion for whom she was the most special person in the world.

Eventually, I confided to two friends that I longed to have a good partner, and they suggested that I go online. I posted my best picture and tried to write an engaging profile. After eleven disappointing days, I received a pleasant note from an interesting man, a recent widower.

Jim hadn't intended to go online, but an ad for a free trial of the site mysteriously popped up on his computer one day. My profile and picture appeared on his screen two days later. As he describes it, he was standing by the internet highway, waiting for a ride my way.

Love Online

The web threads
the vibes
of our lives—

conversation,
commerce,
movies and news,
voices of
a thousand views,
videos, cameos,
goods to retail,
puppies for sale.

Whatever
we desire
can be found
on the wire.

We can even find love.

Of Loss and Love

Bands of love
fly the sky
like morning larks,
when we begin to
open our hearts.

Since we lived a thousand miles apart, Jim in Texas and I in Virginia, we got to know each other first through numerous emails. Jim called this a "courtship of letters." For others online, I recommend becoming well acquainted first in writing, as this was an essential vetting process for me before moving to the next step—meeting in person.

As our relationship developed, I knew that I had a choice: to keep my heart locked up, and continue in my mostly comfortable widow ways, or to open myself, to explore a whole new life with a new partner. I had already nursed one husband in ill health. Would I be willing to care for, sacrifice for another if it came to that later? Life has its way of throwing curve balls as we age.

By this time, Jim was fully committed to our future together. I needed time to reflect.

In My Hand

His heart is
in my hand.
He gave it to me
slowly,
guardedly,
at first.
Then with
full faith and
force.

A profound awareness.

One now has
the power
to crush
another's heart,
another's
hopeful reason
for being.

I pause.
Must think.
He will need space
in my closets as
well as my mind.
We are in too deep
to turn back.

And what of his heart?

I will honor and
cherish it,
hold it
gently always
through our
remaining days.

I have
the power
within
to make
his heart sing.

My adult children naturally questioned their mother's wisdom in embarking on a new romance with a stranger from across the continent, especially someone found online. Then one day I fell in my backyard and broke my arm in two places. I was impaired and needed help, more than my family was capable of giving, with their jobs, children, and numerous other responsibilities.

Jim arrived from the airport at midnight and took over from there, earning the family's trust and friendship.

Footsteps

How fine to hear
footsteps
in the house
again.

I lie in a soft space,
arm in a sling,
wing broken in a
garden tumble.

I was alone,
body prone,
on wet,
slick brick.

Pain, tears.
No one near.
No one to hear.

I found a phone,
a ride to the
emergency room.
A long recovery
ahead.

Of Loss and Love

Before,
days and nights
endured alone.
No more.

My good man
is here.

I note
his presence,
walking softly on
old wood floors,
opening doors,
looking for my
brush and combs.

I rest my wound
on a down pillow,
close my eyes,
and listen
thankfully
for the quiet footsteps.

Home sweet home.

When the holidays approached, we decided to spend Christmas Day with our respective families and then to do something special on New Year's Eve. That night, we watched brilliant bursts of fireworks high above the shining blue waters of Hong Kong harbor. On January 1st, we made plans to be married. To this day, we are amazed by the journey.

ABOUT THE AUTHOR

Following a career in corporate and non-profit communications, Suzanne found time for writing. She is the author of a biography about Founding Father George Wythe, *Jefferson's Godfather: The Man Behind the Man,* and *The Metaphysical Thomas Jefferson.* She lectures frequently on the Jefferson-Wythe legacy.

Forthcoming books are *First in Law, First in Leadership*, the story of America's first law school and school for statesmen at the College of William & Mary, and *The Metaphysical Leonard Cohen.* She and her husband Jim live in Central Virginia. For more information: www.suzannemunson-author.com.

www.ingramcontent.com/pod-product-compliance
Lightning Source LLC
Chambersburg PA
CBHW050748110526
44591CB00002B/13